BREAKING THE CHAINS OF TRAUMA

A 30-Day Devotional for Overcoming Generational Trauma Using the Story of Sojourner Truth

Joyce Marrie, Ph.D.

2nd Edition 2025
1st Edition Copyright© Library of Congress
April 2020. ISBN 978-1-7358122-0-5 Hardcover

Breaking the Chains of Trauma A 30-Day Devotional for Overcoming Generational Trauma Using the Story of Sojourner Truth.

Unless otherwise stated, the scripture references are from the New International Version (NIV), English Standard Version (ESV), King James Version (KJV), Revised Standard Version RSV), New King James Version (NKJV), and Message Bible (MSG)

Published by Chloe Arts and Publishing, LLC
Edited: Dr. Sheryl Grassie

All rights reserved. No portion of this publication may be reproduced, stored in a retrieval system, or transmitted in any form by any means electronic, or mechanical, without the prior written permission of the publisher.

Printed and bound in the United States of America

TABLE OF CONTENTS

Acknowledgment	iv
Author's Notes	v
Preface	vii
Introduction	ix
What is Trauma?	xii
Day 1 Planting Seeds	1
Day 2 New Growth	5
Day 3 In Crisis Mode	9
Day 4 Cries of Grief and Loss	13
Day 5 Falling in Love	17
Day 6 Walking Away	21
Day 7 Shelter in a Storm	25
Day 8 The Cry of a Child	29
Day 9 A Slave (Victim) Mentality	34
Day 10 Deception	38
Day 11 Certificates of Character	42
Day 12 A Loss But Found	46
Day 13 The Inner Voice	50
Day 14 Speak From Your Heart With Wisdom	54
Day 15 Bullied	58
Day 16 Press On	62

Day 17 A Story to be Told	67
Day 18 Opportunities to Prosper	71
Day 19 Barriers Must Come Down	75
Day 20 Selfless Love and	78
the Willingness to Serve	68
Day 21 Speaking Out Against Injustice	81
Day 22 Breaking Ground	85
Day 23 A Test of Character	89
Day 24 Be A Problem Solver	93
Day 25 Feeling Privilege	97
Day 26 Citizenship	101
Day 27 Gaining Territory	105
Day 28 Taking Care of Ourselves	109
So We Can Take Care of Others	96
Day 29 Being Who You Are	112
Day 30 Breaking the Chains	117
In Conclusion	121
In Memory of-	
Saleemah Shabazz Salahud-Din	123
About the Author	124
Biography	125
Sankofa	126

"He saw the need and moved with compassion to heal the broken hearted"

ACKNOWLEDGEMENTS

First and foremost, I want to thank God for His inspiration. Special thanks to my family: Tony, Terry, and Joy, and son-in-law, Brennis.
Thanks to my 100-year-old mom, Mildred Garrett, sisters: Ruth and Loretta, and Darlene, my niece for your love and support!

Thank you to Ed and Regina Irwin, who inspired me to take on the journey of Sojourner Truth, through the re-enactment of the Underground Railroad.

Thanks to Dr. Carolyn Yusuf and Judith Hence.

AUTHOR'S NOTES

When I started writing this devotional, we were in the middle of the spring 2020 Covid-19 pandemic. The virus had already taken the lives of many, and it was heartbreaking. The pain and suffering caused traumatization for many.

During this period of staying at home, our lives seem paused, and time seems to stand still. It presents a wonderful time to listen to our hearts and to reevaluate our lives as God speaks to us. Business stops for a time and leaves us with an opportunity to hear God and know what He is asking us to do.

What He asked of me was this book. I had no conscious thought of writing it. It just started coming to me. I would wake up early in the morning, and He would give me what to write. Just when I thought I completed the book, He would give me more. I knew it was time to break the chains of generational trauma still being suffered by so many in the black community. From slavery to ongoing discrimination, from feeling victimized to living in fear, I realized this was the message of this book.

The world is now at a standstill with this virus, and we are searching for answers. What do we do now? Is there a cure? Will we get back to normal? What will be our new "normal? How are we going to get through this? Fear has gripped the hearts of many, and we feel like there is nowhere to turn. We are lost and looking for an answer.

To compound matters, George Floyd was killed on

Memorial Day in the very neighborhood where I grew up, and my city erupted into "Black Lives Matter" protests and riots. There is a shift taking place in our nation today! God is positioning and commissioning us, and He wants to give us direction for needed change.

I realized that tough times force us to choose between faith in God and living in fear, and we base our actions on which one we choose. I decided to choose faith and help others choose it too. This book motivated me to think about where I am putting my focus and how I can help myself and others. I found my answer: healing by birthing a new vision of how things can be and overcoming the fear of this trauma-inducing world in which we live. God doesn't want us to live in fear.

For me, writing this book has helped me make process in life and have more compassion than before. I am overcoming things, and my hope is that this book will offer healing to others. Just know that He will remove the chains that bind us, we're all in this together. Step into your destiny! We will get through this!

The Scripture gives us assurance in 2 Peter 1: 3-4 (New International Version), "His divine power has given us everything we need for life and godliness through our knowledge of Him who called us by His own glory and goodness. Through these, He has given us His very great and precious promises, so that through Him, we may participate in the divine nature and escape the corruption in the world caused by evil desires."

PREFACE

As a drama therapist, I discovered years ago that "mirroring" can have a powerful therapeutic effect on both actors and audience. Seeing someone else overcome pain and trauma can offer solutions to our anxieties. Sojourner Truth's story provides many opportunities for understanding trauma and suggests ways to move through it. It is critical today to address and find solutions to trauma growing implications in our daily lives.

The biographies of many African Americans demonstrate the trauma and suffering experienced by our ancestors. This trauma lives in our blood and souls and predisposes us to injury in our current lives. It is easy to disregard the past and forget the bridge crossed by our ancestors to be where we are today, but there is both healing and awareness to be gained from revisiting these stories.

The use of a narrative is a powerful way to create a frame of reference. When I look at Sojourner Truth and her life, I see myriads of vignettes within her story that are relevant today. Sojourner's life, her passion, her resiliency, and her devotion to God have inspired me. By retelling her story in a devotional form, this book's purpose is to encourage reflection and inspire
one's spiritual journey. "We're all on a journey
to find the truth."

The zeitgeist in the African American community is to look at generational trauma and essentially how to "break the chains" that keep us stuck in the past with our beliefs and behaviors. Sojourner was not the first African American to experience hardship, nor the first to overcome it. She is a shining example, however, of what one person can rise above and accomplish, and her story is essential for several reasons. Sojourner provides an example, a mirror, of what one can do. She solidly anchors us in a history that runs through our veins and gives us hope for better outcomes in our own lives. She also shows us a path to change by listening to and following God's direction.

This devotional's purpose is to help free you from the trauma or traumatic situations in your life. I hope you will use this book to birth a new vision for your life and know that God hears your cry and will help direct you out of your trauma, no matter how bad it is.

As I am putting the final touches on this manuscript, it is August of 2020, and we are heading into elections in the coming months. This year marks the 100th anniversary of the 19th amendment when women earned the right to vote. Sojourner Truth played an important role in the women's suffrage movement.

INTRODUCTION

About Sojourner Truth

Sojourner Truth, born Isabella Baumfree in 1797, was raised a slave and became an African-American abolitionist and women's rights activist. She lived a long life, well into her 80's, and died in 1883. She initially lived in Ulster County, New York, with her parents, James and Elizabeth (Mau Mau) Baumfree, owned by Colonel Johnnis Hardenbergh, a Revolutionary War colonel. Ulster County was primarily Dutch-speaking, and that was Sojourners' first language. In 1806, when Isabella was nine, she was sold at auction. Speaking only Dutch, she was beaten daily for her inability to communicate with her new owners.

During the years of her enslavement, she was bought and sold five times and suffered extreme conditions and abuse. She was eventually married to another slave named Thomas. She had five children, at least one of which was the result of rape by her owner. Her first son died in childhood, and her remaining three daughters and one son lived into adulthood. In 1826, when she was 29 years old, she escaped with her infant daughter, Sophia, and was taken in by Isaac and Maria Van Wagenen's. They bought her services from her previous owner and supported Sojourner and her daughter until a year later, in 1827, when she gained her freedom.

During her time with the Van Wagenen's, she became deeply religious. In 1828, Isabella went to court to regain custody of her 5-year-old son, Peter, who had been sold illegally. She won her case and gained renown as one of the first black women to win a court case against a white man.

After she regained her son, she spent time working and helping the poor in New York. In 1843, she changed her name to Sojourner Truth as part of a calling to travel and preach about abolition. She gained recognition and began speaking widely and meeting with government officials, including Abraham Lincoln. In 1851, she gave her famous speech, "Ain't I a woman?" at the Ohio Women's Rights Convention. She devoted years of her life to speaking across the country in support of women's rights and the abolition of slavery. From 1857-1867, she lived in a spiritualist community in Harmonia, Michigan, and then settled for the remainder of her life in nearby Battle Creek, Michigan, where she died in 1883.

Sojourner left a legacy of advocating for the rights of African Americans and women's rights issues. As you read and use this story to work through your trauma, I hope that you will discover more about who you are. We all have generational chains that hold us back, whether or not we can see them. Sojourner is a shining example of one of our ancestors who helped pave the way for us to break both the external and internal chains that hold us back in life. She demonstrated this through love and care for others, through her deep faith in God's helping hand, and through strong will and determination.

This daily devotional is not meant to pull us into the past, but to give us more understanding of our roots so we can move forward. Healing can take place when we are mindful of our beginnings and consciously, through faith, discover why we feel this fear, locate it, breathe, and let go of the hidden chains that bind us to the trauma of past generations.

WHAT IS TRAUMA?

The Greek word for trauma translates as a "wound." To the ancient Greeks, trauma was a physical wound, but in more recent centuries, the term 'trauma' often refers to emotional and psychological wounds. Trauma is the response we have to an unpleasant event or series of such events.

Causes of Trauma

- An intense encounter or upsetting experience
- Trauma may result from losing a family member or a loved one.
- Trauma may be related to a single violent experience such as rape, physical abuse, or even a car accident.
- Trauma may result from ongoing abuse, either physical or emotional, or from psychological mistreatment.
- Trauma might be caused by rejection from a parent or partner, loss of a job, or diminished circumstances.

Responses to Trauma

- You may have difficulty functioning and doing normal tasks.
- You may experience an inner emotional struggle.
- You may have heightened reactions to current experiences.

- You may have trouble sleeping or health issues.
- Trauma may be an overwhelming experience, leaving a detrimental memory.
- You could experience ongoing painful memories.
- Your trauma may result in depression or posttraumatic stress disorder (PTSD).

From Trauma to Freedom"

BREAKING THE CHAINS OF TRAUMA

Planting Seeds
Day 1

The things we hear, and think are seeds that grow into beliefs. These beliefs can hinder us or sustain us during difficult times.

In 1797, Sojourner Truth, born Isabella Baumfree, was the twelfth child born to James and Elizabeth Baumfree, slaves owned by Colonel Johnnis Hardenbergh. Most of her brothers and sisters were sold before she was born, the last two while she was an infant. Her parents endured the pain of losing their children one after another.

When their owner, the Colonel died, his son became their new overseer. He moved them from a decent two-bedroom cabin with wood floors and furniture, to an old one-room cabin with dirt floors. It was like a dungeon, perpetually damp, and the only light that came through was from cracks in the walls. At times, when it rained, water would drip through, and the floors would become a muddy mess. During the winter, there was no heat, and the wind would blow through the walls. The family had one blanket to share among the three of them. Food was limited, the work was hard, and the punishment was regular.

Sojourner's mother, however, remained in good spirits despite their difficult circumstances. She would talk about God and say, "He hears and sees all, a brighter day is coming." Her mother would tell stories about Sojourner's brothers and sisters, and then she would cry, but she never lost faith that things would get better. She knew how to make the best of a bad situation, and she planted seeds in Sojourner's thinking, that life always holds the possibility to improve through faith in God.

Think Today

Having a solid faith-based foundation is the key to making it through hard times. There are so many challenges in life that can immobilize us. Our struggles are real, and how we master them depends on what we think and believe. In times of adversity, we must take steps to move forward mentally and physically. I like the expression, "Keep it moving," as a way to remember there are possibilities to create change and experience a healthier life.

Sojourner had words of faith spoken to her over and over as she grew up. These seeds formed into beliefs that sustained her. She carried the words from her mother and used them when faced with her difficulties. Her trust in God saw her through hard times and supported her while she worked with the challenges of being a slave.

It is good to plant seeds of hope in your children and other loved ones. These seeds can develop into a faith that can carry them. We must believe in the power of God and trust that He is willing to carry us through when there doesn't seem to be a way out. Plant seeds in yourself and others. God has a plan, even when we cannot see the way.

Ask Yourself

- What seeds were planted in me? Positive or negative? How do I water the positive ones?

- What seeds am I planting in others? Do I sow seeds of hope and love in my children and those around me? Or do I continue the negative and limiting beliefs that are not of God?

- When I feel challenged, I have a choice of what to believe and what to focus on. What do I choose?

- Do I turn to God for help when I have trouble believing things will be okay? How do I stay connected to God so that He can sustain me?

Bible Passage

"Now faith is the substance of things hoped for, the evidence of things not seen" (Heb. 11:1 King James Version),

Time to Reflect

New Growth
Day 2

Everyone experiences changes throughout their life. These changes can be welcomed or unwelcomed, but you are the only person who can determine what you will make of your new circumstances.

Since all of Sojourner's siblings had been sold before her, her parents worried her master would sell her as well. In 1806, at the age of nine, Sojourner was sold on the auction block, along with a flock of sheep. She was shackled and inspected like one of the herds, her clothes half ripped off, men looking into her ears and mouth, inspecting her backside, all in front of a crowd that regarded her as nothing more than a piece of property.

There were no takers for some time, and it looked as if Sojourner would not be sold. Then a slave owner named John Neely shouted, "If you throw in some of the sheep, I'll take her," and the sale was made. Isabella's pain and humiliation burned as she was loaded into a wagon and forced to watch as her mother cried in agony. She had no idea where she was going or what lay in store. On top of that, her new master did not speak Dutch.

Neely was cruel and continually beat Sojourner for not understanding English. Being a young girl of nine, being taken from her parents, and placed in a home where she didn't understand what her owner requested of her, and why she was abused physically and emotionally, was very traumatizing, even if it was "normal" for the times.

Sojourner had to change and adapt to her new circumstances. She did not have the support of her parents; she had to learn a new language and navigate the harsh environment. She only had God as a source of comfort in those difficult times.

Think Today

Even today, life can be unpredictable. Our happiness is connected to how much control we have over our lives, and when times are uncertain, or things happen that are beyond our control, it can be very upsetting.

When we think of the pain that both Sojourner and her parents endured, it is unimaginable. It is unthinkable to have a child taken against your will and sold. Sojourner's mother must have spent long hours missing her child, remembering their times together, and concerned about what was happening to her.

Imagine the trauma of living a life where you had no control, where someone else determined where you lived and how you lived. How did Sojourner and her parents make it through? Did their faith make a difference in how they adapted to their changed circumstances?

Ask Yourself

- Have I had times when things were out of our control? Times when I felt powerless? What did that feel like? Was I sad, angry, or uncertain?

- Can I remember a time when life changed unexpectedly? Was it pleasant or traumatic? What did I draw on to help me through it?

- Did I draw on my faith to get through it, or did I experience new growth?

- What would I like to do the next time life changes differently in ways I don't like?

Bible Passage

"So do not fear, for I am with you; do not be dismayed, for I am your God. I will strengthen you and help you; I will uphold you with my righteous right hand" (Isa. 41:10 NIV).

Time to Reflect

In Crisis Mode
Day 3

When we operate out of anxiety or depression, we limit ourselves. Crisis and loss are a part of life that can be managed with God's help.

After Sojourner was sold, she was still able to keep in touch with her parents. In the State of New York, a law was passed that freed slaves over the age of 50. Her parents were over the age of 50 and qualified for their freedom. They had no money, however, and had to remain working for their owner. Her father was old and crippled by this time and could not work, but Sojourner's mother was able to work to support them. Their quality of life was extremely poor, still living in a rat-infested, dirt-floor cabin with no windows.

Sojourner was disturbed by their conditions but was helpless to do anything about it. Her mother became sick and died, and this was very upsetting for young Sojourner. Two other slaves moved into the cabin with her father, who began to deteriorate after his wife's death. Mr. Neely allowed Sojourner to visit her father, and she found him in terrible shape, heartbroken, and crying. He had fallen into a terrible depression.

Sojourner tried to pull him out of his despair with talk of the new law that might be passed that would free all slaves. Then she could come back and take care of him. After her visit, he stopped eating and ultimately died. Sojourner was devastated because her father gave up on living. She felt helpless and alone after losing both of her parents, she too fell into hopelessness.

Think Today

When we lose a loved one or face a crisis, we tend to experience fear, anxiety, anger, grief, and loss or depression. There is uncertainty about what will happen next and how we will get through it. Often how we respond to these circumstances can determine the outcome. If we allow depression to take over, it can wear on our spirits, creating more anxiety.

Thankfully, in today's world, depression is treatable. Sojourner had no choice but to find a way through it on her own. She could draw on the words of her mother, who always said the future would be brighter, and told her God is here to help. We all have an opportunity to ask for help. Even when things are seemingly bleak, God is there to guide us through. His strength and wisdom can carry us through any crisis if we allow Him to.

Ask Yourself

- Am I in a crisis or suffering from anxiety? How am I dealing with it?

- Am I worrying about things over which I don't have control? Who is my comforter?

- Am I asking for help?

- Am I connected to God and allowing Him to support me?

Bible Passage

"Do not be anxious about anything, but in everything by prayer and supplication with thanksgiving, let your request be made known to God, and the peace of God which transcends all understanding. Will guard your hearts and your minds in Christ Jesus" (Phil. 4:6-7)

Time to Reflect

Cries of Grief and Loss
Day 4

Sojourner kept her mother's faith alive in her heart, which helped her through difficult times as she was bought and sold, raped, beaten, and lost her first-born child.

Sojourner had to bear much of her trauma and grief alone. She had little time to reflect or process because she worked extremely hard and lived in very harsh conditions. She resided for two years with the man who bought her and took her from her parents, John Neely. Sojourner described him as cruel, and her years as his slave were very punitive. She had to bear the trauma of leaving her family, being sold, living where a different language was spoken, and daily beatings that were extreme.

Still, Sojourner did have her parents' love and her faith in God. She believed that things could get better, and they did. She was sold again to Martinus Schryver, a tavern keeper who owned her for 18 months. Then she was sold to John Dumont, and although he was a kinder master, his wife disliked and harassed Sojourner, and she was raped repeatedly by Dumont.

Sojourner gave birth to a son James, her firstborn when she was a young teen. James died as a child. Imagine how heartbroken she must have been. But there was no time to work through her pain. Slaves were told to be quiet, and they had to keep things inside. Sojourner often thought of her mother and how she prayed in times of struggle. It was hard for her to keep the pain inside, although she received encouragement from the other slave women.

Some years later, in 1815, at the age of 18, Sojourner had a second child, a daughter, Diana, either fathered by Dumont, or possibly another slave with whom she was in love. She was then married off to a slave named Thomas, a much older man who she did not love or even know very well. The overseers chose who their slaves married. Sojourner had three additional children with Thomas- Peter in 1821, Elizabeth in 1825, and Sophia in 1826.

Think Today

We all have painful experiences while growing up. Sometimes we hide from, or cover-up those unhealthy memories, giving ourselves no time for healing. Over time, unhealed wounds can get triggered, causing us to snap or reach a breaking point.

When there is no heart-to-heart dialogue within us about our pain, or someone to help us work it through, or if we do not take the time to process and grieve, pain and suffering can escalate. In our culture, we are told to "get over it." But we do not get over trauma quickly. It needs to be felt, understood, forgiven, and resolved. Otherwise, it will continue to repeat itself from generation to generation. We live in a time where every one of us has experienced a loss of some kind or another.

Ask Yourself

- When was the last time I experienced a traumatic loss? Did I allow myself to feel it? To grieve it?

- Was there someone to help me through the pain? Do I have someone I can turn to, talk to, and from whom I can receive empathy? Have I asked for God's help?

- Have my own children suffered trauma? Have I been there for them?

- Am I in denial of the truth and covering up my pain from the past? Have I let myself grieve for painful things that have happened? Have I made peace with the past so I can more fully live in the present?

Bible Passage

"The Lord is close to the brokenhearted and saves those who are crushed in spirit" (Ps. 34:18).

Time to Reflect

Falling in Love
Day 5

Love opens our hearts to the potential for both great joy and great loss. When love turns to loss, it can mean pain and trauma. We must work through that pain. Loving relationships are gifts from God, and He is here to help us through them.

Before Sojourner was married to Thomas, and after the death of her first child James, she fell deeply in love with a slave named Robert. They lived in separate plantations, which made it difficult for them to see each other. Robert would sneak away to meet Sojourner, but when his master found out, Robert was beaten and forbidden to see her.

The overseers at that time did not want slaves from different plantations mixing. They wanted female slaves to bear children on their plantation, with no dispute about who fathered the children questioning if the child belonged to another plantation owner. Slave children were property for work or to be sold for profit.

Robert continued to see Isabella, disobeying his overseer. One day, he was caught and beaten unmercifully, then hauled away. Sojourner was watching this from a window. One version of the story says he was beaten by the overseer so severely that he died from his injuries. Another version says he recovered and was married off to a slave from a different plantation but died a few years later from all the physical abuse he suffered. Either way, Sojourner never saw him again after that day.

Around this time in 1815, Sojourner gave birth to her second child, Diana, who was either the result of being raped by her owner, John Dumont, or was Roberts's child.

Think Today

Love can create a euphoria that makes loss extremely painful. Having a great love torn away, as Sojourner did, created a massive void in her life. It may have been filled in part by the birth of her daughter, but Sojourner was never to get over the loss of Robert fully, and she mourned him throughout her life.

Whether a relationship ends out of choice because of circumstances, or even death, it creates feelings of loneliness and uncertainty. The void it creates can leave us feeling angry or bitter, which may lead to depression. Although we may not see a way out, there is hope in every situation. You can free yourself from the pain of loss by forgiveness and by not allowing the pain to grow roots. Let go of what happened and how it made you feel. Talk to God about it and let his love fill the void.

Ask Yourself

- Do I feel violated and hurt by a broken relationship or the death of a loved one?

- Am I emotionally drained and don't know what to do?

- Do I continue to waver in a dysfunctional relationship, unable to decide whether to stay or leave?

- Am I allowing myself to heal before entering a new relationship?

Bible Passage

"Cast all your anxiety on Him because he cares for you" (1 Pet. 5:7).

Time to Reflect

Walking Away
Day 6

There are times we must be brave and walk away from a bad situation. In 1826, Sojourner walked away from her life as a slave and sought freedom and a better life.

In 1824, when Sojourner was 27 years old, she became aware of a law passed in 1817 that freed slaves born before 1799. The legislation would emancipate these slaves, but not until July 4, 1827. It required that male slaves must be over the age of 28 and female slaves over 25. She had been praying that she would be free one day, and this news felt like an answer to her prayers. After hearing the good news, she sang, danced, and gave thanks.

She then spoke with Mr. Dumont about gaining her freedom. He promised her that she could be free earlier if she worked extra hard. Sojourner did work extremely hard, but she sustained an injury to her finger. This injury became an excuse for Mr. Dumont to renege on his promise, saying it hindered the quality of her work.

Sojourner was so furious that she decided to run away. In 1826, when she was 29, and after giving birth to her fifth child, Sojourner chose to leave the abuse and seek freedom. Fearful of fleeing in the night, she left just before dawn with her baby Sophia in her arms. She was heartbroken to leave her other children, but she knew they would be well taken care of by the other slaves, and she would reunite with them as soon as possible.

Think Today

Sojourner had to take a risk to move to a better life. What would it mean to move from being owned by someone else, having her life dictated by another, to freedom and the right to make her own choices? God created us sovereign beings with dominion over our thoughts, our bodies, and our actions.

It took strength and courage for Sojourner to leave her family and set out on her own with an infant. She had to find great inner strength and trust in God. When she left, she had nowhere to go. It could have ended badly. Runaway slave catchers could have caught her and returned her to the Dumont, but Sojourner took the risk, and with great risk comes great opportunity.

Sojourners' actions are a metaphor for all of us. She teaches by her leaving that we can all walk away from bad situations. Most of us, if we left a bad job or a bad relationship, would not be risking at the level Sojourner did, and yet we are afraid. We can take faith over fear and inspiration from her actions and ask God to help us find the strength to create change.

Ask Yourself

- Where do I feel enslaved in my life?

- From what people or situations do I need to walk away?

- Can I trust that God will lead me to something better? Can I find the strength to do what I need to do?

- What holds me back from risking? What holds me back from letting go of the old and safe way of doing things and moving to something new and better?

Bible Passages

"The LORD is a stronghold for the oppressed, a stronghold in times of trouble. And those who know your name put their trust in you, for you, O LORD, have not forsaken those who seek you" (Ps. 9:9-10 English Standard Version).

"Come to me, all who labor and are heavy laden, and I will give you rest. Take my yoke upon you and learn from me, for I am gentle and slowly in heart, and you will find rest for your souls. For my yoke is easy, and my burden is light" (Matt. 11:28-30 New King James Version).

Time to Reflect

Shelter in a Storm
Day 7

Whenever we are in need, God will provide. All we have to do is ask and listen and follow His directions.

Alone on the road, tired and in need of shelter, Sojourner prayed for help. She remembered a farmer, Levy Row, and made her way to his farm. Unfortunately, he was ill and could not help her, but he directed her to some kindly neighbors, the Van Wagenen's. They gladly took her in and were both amazed by her story and determined to help her. They allowed her to stay, offered her a safe home, and gave her employment as their housekeeper.

Mr. Dumont, however, never gave up looking for Isabella and eventually arrived at the Van Wagenen intent on taking Sojourner and her daughter back to his farm. Mr. Van Wagenen stepped in and defended Sojourner, offering a fair price for her and Sophia; he knew if she went back, she would be beaten for leaving. Not only did Mr. Van Wagenen offer her a safe place to live, but he also paid for her freedom.

Sojourner worked for and lived with the Van Wagenen's for roughly three years. She took their last name and felt part of their family.
She officially gained her freedom status in 1827, a year after moving in with the Van Wagenen's.

Think Today

Isabella experienced a period of homelessness with her child, not knowing where to go and looking for shelter. It must have been traumatic to be poor, alone, a black slave fleeing from an unkind owner with no place to go and an infant in your arms. How traumatizing!

We live in a society where more and more people are lost and looking for stability and a home. Homelessness is rampant, with too many people wondering about where their next meal will come from. Homeless shelters are overcrowded, leaving many people reduced to sleeping under bridges or in abandoned buildings.

In modern times, our storms are different. Maybe you cannot pay your mortgage or rent and are being evicted. Perhaps you do not know where your next meal will come from. Perhaps you are in an unhealthy relationship and have to leave your home.

Storms come in many different forms, and we all need shelter. There are many reasons individuals may be seeking comfort and not sure where to go or what to do. Just remember, there is always a light at the end of the tunnel.
God sees you and knows where you are. You can look to Him for help.

Ask Yourself

- Have I been through a tough time when I needed "shelter from a storm?"

- Is my home a place of comfort, peace, or stability? And one that I share with others in need?

- Am I sensitive to others when they are in impoverished situations?

- Have I ever helped or taken in a homeless person?

Bible Passage

"And there shall be a tabernacle for a shadow in the daytime from the heat, and for a place of refuge, and for a covert from storm and from rain" (Isa. 4:6).

Time to Reflect

The Cry of a Child
Day 8

Inside of Sojourner's heart, she could hear the anguished cries of the children she had left behind, especially Peter, the deep pain of having been separated from her parents at a young age resonated with her. Although she might have chosen to ignore these cries, she found the strength to do what was necessary.

Sojourner missed the children she had left behind. Fortunately, she had a network of other slaves, who would get word to her about how they were doing. Through this network, she heard that her five-year-old son Peter had been illegally sold from the Dumont farm to a man named Solomon Gedney and ended up on a plantation in Alabama.

This news was especially upsetting to Sojourner because Alabama was in the South. Unlike New York, it did not have any emancipation laws, meaning her son would be a slave forever if she did not do something.

Sojourner refused to stand by to watch injustice unfold. Determined to take action, she approached the Dumont for answers. Mr. Dumont insisted he was unaware that Peter had been taken South, while his wife dismissively laughed and resorted, "Why are you worrying about one black child? That callous remark ignited a fire resolve in Sojourner, strengthening her determination to pursue her son.

Sojourner was able to meet with the Gedneys to try and regain her son. They rejected her request and dismissed her. Sojourner did not let that rejection affect her resolve or dampen her spirit. She continued to ask God how she could get her son back. She reached out to the Quaker friends she knew through the Van Wagenen's who often helped slaves. They advised her to file a lawsuit against Solomon Gedney. They helped raise donations to pay for a lawyer, and Sojourner was able to get a court hearing. It took many months, but in the end, she won the case, and the judge ordered Solomon Gedney to give Peter back to his mother.

In 1827, it was unheard of for a black woman to take a white man to court, but with the help of the Lord and her Quaker friends, Sojourner was able to step into that courtroom and fight for her son.

Think Today

Many parents can hear the cries of their children and feel their pain. They will also fight for their children. Sojourner could feel her child's pain and see his bleak future if she did nothing.

Children crave protection from their parents, both physically and emotionally. Parents are their protectors. But not all of us were protected as children. The lack of protection leaves us feeling angry, confused, and caught between sadness and hope. Without a positive modal of nurturing and resilience in our own upbringing, we may struggle to provide the same support and guidance for our children. Many of us grew up without strong determined parents that would fight for us and do the right thing, leaving us feeling angry, confused, and caught between sadness and hopelessness.

Without positive nurturing and resilience in our own upbringing, we might struggle to provide the same support and guidance for our children.

It is not too late to change. We can all learn from Sojourner's bravery and determination to help her child.

Ask Yourself

. Reflect on memories and identify opportunities where you could have responded differently. It's not about dwelling on mistakes but recognizing areas of growth.

- If I have children, am I listening to their cries? Do I regret how I raised my child or children?

  .

- Have I thought about myself as a child? How was I treated? Did someone fight for me?

- Have I made up for any deficits in my childhood?

- Am I willing to help other children who aren't protected? Those in troubling situations or experiencing trauma?

Compare how you respond to challenges now and how you did in the past. Do you find that you are now more resilient or capable of providing support for yourself and others?

Bible Passage

"But when Jesus saw it, He indignant, and said to them, 'Let the children come to me; do not hinder them, for to such belongs the kingdom of God' (Mark 10:14 Revised Standard Version).

Time to Reflect

A Slave (Victim) Mentality
Day 9

We can change our circumstances, but if we do not change the way we think, we will recreate our problems in a new place. Peter moved to a new home, but he had a hard time leaving his slave mentality behind.

Peter was frightened when brought to court, and he held tight to Solomon Gedney, his overseer. He was afraid to identify his mother because Gedney had threatened him. The Judge asked him about a scar on his forehead, and rather than tell the truth, out of fear, Peter lied to protect Gedney. Letting go of being controlled by a master was hard for Peter, and he went to his mother screaming and kicking. Sojourner understood that the scars on his back were signs of repeated brutal beatings.

Peter stayed with his mother at the Van Wagen's for several years while she continued to work for them. They had a strong faith in God and would often read the Bible to Sojourner and Peter. Life with the Van Wagenen's was a much better for him, one filled with love and care. But the experiences during his years as a slave left deep scars. As he got older, he began to steal, and when caught stealing, he would lie.

Sojourner moved Peter and his younger sister Sophia to New Your City in 1829. In New York, Peter had the opportunity for education and to learn a trade. Unfortunately, he would take one step forward and one back, starting an education but getting involved with a rough crowd and getting into trouble. Despite his changed and improved circumstances, Peter had not let go of the pain and trauma from his childhood, and that pain led him to make bad choices and engage in harmful behavior later in life.

Think Today

Destructive behavior is a function of underlying emotional problems. As Frederick Douglass said, "It's better to build strong children than to repair broken men." When others maltreat us, we form beliefs about ourselves and develop unhealthy ways of seeing the world. This unhealthy view of life can lead to patterns of behavior like the ones Peter struggled with all of his life. The beatings he received as a young child, the role of a slave, and the life slavery required, left deep scars.

Although Peter's circumstances continued to change for the better, and despite the love and opportunities that came his way, he had a mindset that led him to engage in unhealthy behaviors. This victim mindset caused Peter to sabotage his new life.
Interacting with others may have caused him anxiety, and feelings of being powerless may have interfered with his doing well in school or work.
How many times do we find this same victim mindset of our children today, who are traumatized by seeing violence or being violated? Some children take on the role of their parents, seeing them in their own struggle and not knowing how to deal with it.

Ask Yourself

- When things are not working in my life, do I change my circumstances and take my destructive beliefs with me? Or do I change how I think?

- How do I see myself? Do I see myself as a victim?

- When things improve in my life, do I sabotage them because I have not let go of old beliefs and experiences?

- Have I dealt with past hurts and trauma? Do they sometimes come outside as bad behavior or how do I deal with my own children?

. Have you noticed certain triggers that bring up old wounds? Do you sometimes react to ways that surprise you or feel disproportionate to the situations? If so, that doesn't mean you're failing, it means there's something within that still needs healing.

Bible Passage

"And do not be conformed to this world but be transformed by the renewing of your mind, that you may prove what is that good and acceptable, and perfect will of God" (Rom. 12:2 NKJV).

Time to Reflect

Deception
Day 10

Being lied to or deceived is a part of life. Learning to be honest, learning who to trust, and being able to trust our perceptions of other people is an essential part of living a healthy life.

After moving to New York City, Sojourner worked as a housekeeper for Elijah Pierson, an evangelical Christian preacher. She also volunteered at the Magdalene Asylum, a place that provided food and shelter for homeless girls. As part of his ministry, Elijah Pierson, who was the director, would go out and find girls in absolutely destitute situations and care for them at the Asylum. Sojourner would help by teaching the girls cooking, sewing, and by today's standards, entrepreneurial skills.

Through Elijah Pierson, Sojourner met a charismatic minister, Prophet Matthias, who asked Sojourner and Elijah Pierson to follow him to Zion Hill, New York, and offered Sojourner a housekeeping job. Prophet Matthias was abusive and controlling, dictating people's beliefs, diets, and sexual partners. He broke up marriages and reassigned people into different couples. Sojourner revered Matthias and gave him money from her savings. Although numerous people warned her that he was not to be trusted, she was blind to his deceptive ways.

Elijah Pierson became sick and began to deteriorate. Prophet Matthias refused him any medical care relying only on prayer. One evening, Elijah ate a large number of blackberries and became severely ill. He was left to die in his room. The autopsy ruled it death from poisoning.

Even though the police accused Matthias of killing Elijah, Sojourner defended him in court and used up her savings on attorney fees. An affluent member of the Matthias community, Benjamin Folger, spread lies about Sojourner's involvement in Elijah Pierson's death. Sojourner sued him for slander, and to the surprise of many, she won the case. The court ordered Folger to pay her $125, a significant sum at the time. Even more significant was the fact that a poor, black, and uneducated woman won against a rich, educated, white man.

Think Today

Sojourner wanted to believe Prophet Matthias and so deceived herself. Matthias deceived his followers. Folger spread lies about Sojourner. A lie begets another lie, and soon deception can lead to far greater wrongs. Only the truth can set us free.

Many people are deceived because they would rather believe a lie than accept the truth. Deceptions can be "mind games" played on one another. We all have experienced manipulation, been taken advantage of, or taken advantage of others.

The Bible tells us 'not to be deceived.' If you detect something wrong or get a gut feeling that something is not right or is not true, question it. Nine times out of ten, if you ask to know the truth and check in your heart for what is real, you will know.

Ask Yourself

•   Where in my life am I not telling the truth? Where am I intentionally or unintentionally deceiving others?

•   Why is it easy to believe a lie? Why do we fall into deception with others? Why do we deceive ourselves?

We fall into deception with others because we crave connections, validation, and security. Sometimes, we overlook red flags because we want something to be true so badly that we convince ourselves, manipulation or our own past wounds make us more susceptible to believing what isn't real.

•   Can I start by being honest with myself about any deception in my life?

•   Am I willing to tell the truth and make things right with others?

Bible Passage

"Whoever walks in integrity walks securely, but he who makes his ways crooked will be found out" (Prov. 10:9 NIV).

Time to Reflect

Certificates of Character
Day 11

Words carry power, they shape identity, influence perception, and build trust. Words used to describe us are what make up our character. They form a whole that is what people relate to. Sojourner was considered an honest, hardworking woman of integrity, and this served her well when she needed help.

Sojourner may have been too trusting and was deceived easily by Prophet Matthias. But this was born out of the fact that she herself had such high integrity that she could
not imagine others being dishonest. A significant factor in her winning defamation lawsuit was that people wrote letters of character reference extolling her integrity, and that swayed the judge.

Mr. Folger questioned Sojourner's integrity she fought back. She drew on her faith and the support of others. Her life was profiled through the references she received from others. Both her former owner, Mr. Dumont, and her former employees, Mr. Van Wagenen's, gave formal depositions as to her faithful and honest character, her hardworking nature, and how all who knew her spoke well of her. The integrity with which Sojourner lived her life came full circle and helped her out when she needed it.

Think Today

Integrity and sound moral character are essential in establishing a good life. How people perceive us, and how they portray us to others, forms the basis for work references, character references, and the example we set for our children and others. Do people perceive us as kind, caring, and honest? Or are we hurtful, difficult, and unreliable?

Every day, we express who we are through our words and deeds. If life is a stage, we might ask ourselves what character we play. Some characters are known for their humor, and some are grim, loud, or quiet in their projection. Some characters are known for their unpleasant demeanor, always playing the role of an antagonist. Some are hard to work with or difficult to be around with. Character is who you are when no one but God is looking. We have our best life when we live with integrity and work on maintaining a pleasant and loving character.

Ask Yourself

- How would I characterize myself? What are the top five adjectives I would use to describe my character?

- How do I think others would describe me? What are the top five adjectives they would use to describe me in a letter of recommendation?

- Have I given thought to the example I set in the world? Am I loving, kind, and giving, even to strangers?

- Am I asking God to help me build a good character?

Bible Passage

"For this very reason, make every effort to supplement your faith with virtue, and virtue with knowledge, and knowledge with self-control, and self-control with steadfastness, and steadfastness with godliness, and godliness with brotherly affection, and brotherly affection with love. For if these qualities are yours and are increasing, they keep you from being ineffective or unfruitful in the knowledge of our Lord Jesus Christ" (2 Pet. 1:5-8 ESV).

Time to Reflect

A Loss But Found
Day 12

Loss is a part of life. One of the significant losses of Sojourner's life was not having grown up with her sisters and brothers. She was so young when the last two were sold to another slave owner that she didn't have any memories, just the stories her mother told her. However, the hope she held in her heart rewarded her with a surprise reunion.

After 1834, Sojourner moved back into New York City and with her children, attended the Zion Church. It was there she met a woman named Sophia, who looked a lot like her, and when they explored the resemblance, they found they were siblings.

This reunion was an overwhelming experience for Sojourner, marked by tears and lots of emotion. It brought back memories of her mother and father, and the pain of slavery. Another younger sibling, Michael, had been sold at the same time as Sophia, and he was also a member of the Zion Church. This unplanned family reunion was a surprising moment for all of them. They hugged, cried, and shared their experiences.

Her siblings told Sojourner about another sister, Nancy, who had recently died.
She had also been a member of the Zion Church, and Sojourner had known her, but did not know that they were related. Sojourner did not pick up on any family resemblance. It was astounding to think she had sat

with, sang with, and interacted with a woman who was actually her sister. Peter, Sojourner's son, was delighted to have more family, and Sojourner was amazed at the way God answered her prayers by leading her to the Zion Church.

Think Today

Sojourner learned a valuable lesson when she met her lost siblings: That God was directing her life and always working to answer her prayers. Sojourner was already a woman of faith, but this experience deepened it further. It also brought her much joy to be with her family. Her mother's words that "things will get better," echoed in her memory.

For us, family is vital. How we bond with our parents and siblings, whether or not, we learn to build healthy relationships, and it is of the essence if we can put differences aside and have an enjoyable experience. We must stay open and be forgiving. We must mend fences while our loved ones are still alive. We must not allow family dynamics affect our ability to mend relationships while we still have the chance.

Ask Yourself

- Do I have sisters and brothers that I have not seen for a while?

- Am I holding grudges or not willing to forgive a sister or brother?

- Do I have sisters or brothers that I don't even know?

- Have I tried to rectify an estranged relationship with a sibling or friend.

Bible Passage

"Let brotherly love continue" (Heb. 13:1 KJV).

"And above all things have fervent charity among yourselves: for charity shall cover the multitude of sins" (2 Pet. 4:8)

Time to Reflect

The Inner Voice
Day 13

**Everyone has an inner voice that can guide them in the right direction. This voice is connected to God and can offer one a more positive path. Fear, trauma, or external noise can drown out the inner wisdom.
There are stories of individuals who followed their inner voice, and it led them toward healing. Sojourner was able to listen and follow the direction of her inner voice.**

By 1843, Sojourner's children were grown and on their own, and things began to change for her. She was 46 years old and a mature woman who knew and trusted her inner voice. She felt a calling and heard God tell her to preach the truth. She became a Methodist and changed her name from Isabella (her birth name) to Sojourner Truth. She felt called to preach God's word and to educate people about the abolition of slavery. She left New York on a mission to spread the word. She went on foot, traveling north, with only a pillowcase full of belongings. She took practical steps through prayer meditation, and stillness to connect to the inner voice.

Her journey had many challenges, but people were receptive to her sermons. Guided by her inner voice, she lived by a creed that, "God is not the author of confusion, but of love and destroying the evils of the world." She was determined to help people change their minds about slavery, which she saw as evil. She wanted to help former slaves let go of their "slave mentality." Sojourner also had to work to keep her own spirit positive and not be taken down by negative thoughts. As a soldier in God's army, she was fighting for her rights and the rights of others, and maintaining her persistent stand, she was victorious!

Think Today

We live in a world with so many distractions, making it hard to experience calm and quietness and to find the time and place to listen to our inner voice. When we pray, we talk to God, and when we meditate, we listen to God. Sojourner was able to hear God and get direction on how to live her life. She would say to her audience, "I speak to God, and He speaks to me," and people were baffled by her statements and her faith.

Sojourner's ability to overcome her circumstances, and to find a purpose for her life, was a testament to her strength and to her ability to listen. God directed her to take risks and to follow a path of helping others. This path is available to all of us. If we listen and act upon what we hear, we can have a much more purpose-driven life. Cultivate a stronger connection.

Ask Yourself

- Who or what am I listening to make decisions in my life? Am I allowing other people's points of view to distract me from my purpose?
- Can you think of a time that you were guided?

- What is my mission, and how am I bringing it forth?

- Do I have a belief system in God, and do I stand on his Truth?

- How am I feeding my spirit? Am I praying meditating or journaling?

Bible Passage

"Give ear and hear my voice. Listen and hear my words" (Isa. 28:23 NIV).

Time to Reflect

Speak From Your Heart With Wisdom Day 14

Words Have power. The way we speak to others matters. Sometimes we don't think before we speak and can regret what we say. Sojourner set an example of how to speak from the heart and with wisdom. She embodied the ability to speak with conviction she didn't just react, she spoke with purpose, using her voice to uplift, challenge, and inspire.

Sojourner continued to travel and preach. She was a great orator, who could captivate and motivate her audiences. At the same time, she was accessible, and people could relate to her. She often spoke with humor and was not afraid of telling the truth. She had a nurturing way of referring to her audiences as children, calling them "honey, baby, or sweetie." People found this endearing and gravitated to Sojourner, taking in her message. This fact was important because she was largely preaching to white people.

Sojourner struggled with her ability to embrace her audiences fully. She thought to herself, "These white folks have abused me, beaten me, and abused my people, but I can love them, as God would have me do." She would talk about this kind of love and acceptance in her sermons.

Other times, she would speak against racism, saying, "Children, who made your skin white? Was it not

God? Who made mine black? Was it not the same God? Now, children, remember what Sojourner Truth has told you- get rid of your prejudice and learn to love colored people, that you may all be the children of your Father in Heaven."

Think Today

The Bible refers to the way Sojourner tried to communicate as "speaking the truth in love." She was able to confront her audience and be kind at the same time. It took work on her part to bring forth her message in a clear way without being angry with those that had mistreated her. She spoke from a heartfelt place and a place of wisdom that sets a beautiful example for all of us.

There is an old saying, "If you don't have anything good to say, then don't say anything at all." What does this mean? People sometimes struggle with this statement because they think it means they have to lie in order to say nice things. What this statement demands are for us to think before we speak, not to speak unkindly to anyone when it is not necessary, and to recognize if we are gossiping or being hurtful with our words. We should know if we are speaking from intimidation, pain, or low self-esteem. When we are aware of our motivations, our words can come from wisdom.

Ask Yourself

- Do I remember to ask myself if what I am saying will help or hurt the other person?

- Can I step back and think before I speak?

- Can I choose to "say nothing at all?"

- Am I asking God for the wisdom to speak from love?

Bible Passage

"But speaking the truth in love may grow up into him in all things, which is the head, even Christ" (Eph. 4:15 KJV).

Love does not rejoice in unrighteousness but rejoices with the truth. For charity rejoiceth not in iniquity, but rejoiceth in the truth" (1 Cor. 13:6).

Love is glad when truth is spoken-The aim is for Love to display truth.

Time to Reflect

Bullied
Day 15

Bullying is a form of abuse done to another person. Sojourner experienced bullying, but she taught us how to face it, stand up against it, and not let it take us down.

During her travels, Sojourner did not always meet with friendly audiences, and at times, she was heckled and bullied. She was a woman in her 50s and as she traveled from place to place, usually on foot, she had little to protect her. She was preaching to a primarily white audience, often reluctant to be taught by a black woman. Many felt Sojourner was ignorant and uneducated and being a woman did not merit their listening. She would combat these negative attitudes by saying things like, "I know how it is to be taken into a barn, tied to a bar, and beaten till the blood from my back runs down into the hay at my feet."

If she encountered a terribly angry and bullying crowd, she would try singing to help calm the mood. That would often quiet them down a little, and afterward, she could preach to them. Some of the people who bullied her shut up quickly, some left, and others stayed and put down their clubs and listened to what she had to say.
She could often interject a lot of humor that kept people engaged and tamed those who would bully her.

At one particular talk in Syracuse, New York, an abolitionist, George Thompson, gave his speaking engagement over to Sojourner. The audience was not receptive and laughed and booed her. She won them over by saying, "I'll tell you what Mr. Thompson was going to say. He is going to argue that poor Negroes ought to be out of slavery and in the heavenly state of freedom. But children, because I want to keep the white folks who hold slaves from getting sent to hell, I'm asking you to give equal rights to Negros."

Think Today

Sojourner was incredibly brave to take the risks she did. She was taunted, threatened, booed, and publicly humiliated. She experienced fear and pain, but she did not let it stop her. She stayed focused on the mission God had called her to do.

Bullying is serious. It can be extremely hurtful to the person getting bullied. It can come in the form of unwanted aggressive behavior that is physical or verbal. It can range from direct threats to spreading gossip about someone. Bullying behavior happens in the family, in schools, at jobs, in churches, and even in the media. Bullying is about power and control.

Today, bullying can be far more subtle. It can be inappropriate comments, sexual innuendo, or things written on social media. We see examples in the media when they call different leaders stupid or incompetent. Spreading lies is bullying, and creating an "us versus them" mentality is bullying. When it comes to bullying behavior, there is an old saying, "What goes around, comes around." In other words, what you do to someone else, good or bad, will come back to you in some form.

Ask Yourself

- Have I been bullied, or am I a bully?

- Am I a person that stands by and watches while others are being bullied? Who do I know that is a bully?

- Am I one who follows the crowd by agreeing with mean comments about other people?

- Do I hold myself accountable for the way I speak about and act towards others?

Stand up against this behavior and do not let it take you down. Be resilient in the face of bullying.

Bible Passage

"Do not let any unwholesome talk come out of your mouths, but only what is helpful for building others up according to their needs, that it may benefit those who listen" (Eph. 4:29 NIV).

If possible, as far as it depends on you, live at peace with everyone.

Time to Reflect

Press On
Day 16

The ability to press on, to keep moving forward is essential if you hope to succeed. Obstacles that appear are always surmountable with perseverance, patience, and trust in God.

In 1850, Sojourner experienced an obstacle in her work. It came in the form of the Fugitive Slave Act passed in September of that year. This new law allowed for the capture of slaves who had run away and made it north to freedom. They could be apprehended on only the hearsay of a white person and were not allowed a trial. Harsh penalties of hefty fines and prison terms were set up for anyone helping slaves escape. This period was at the height of the Underground Railroad when more and more slaves were making their way north to freedom.

During this time, Sojourner began speaking out more and more about the need to abolish slavery. She was fortunate to have support from others who did not believe in the Fugitive Slave Act. There were many abolitionists, including Frederick Douglass and William L. Garrison, who helped her as she pressed on. Sojourner was invited to speak at a women's rights convention in Massachusetts, where she was the only black woman present. She was one in a lineup of famous speakers, but after she spoke, her words were so impactful that the audience was stunned.

Think Today

In every life, as in every journey, some setbacks and roadblocks require us to "press on" despite them. Every setback is an opportunity to grow stronger. Sojourner found the strength to press on with help from God and the many people that supported her mission. Her circumstances were not easy, and she was often the only woman speaking at a time when women had almost as few rights as slaves. She faced angry crowds, threats, and intimidation from people who did not think she had the right to speak, and at times, some people were so threatening that she feared for her life. Despite these obstacles, Sojourner had a passion for what she did that allowed her to press on.

Pressing on or continuing to move forward towards our goals takes determination and perseverance. It is easy to get derailed by things that happen; setbacks can leave us discouraged and wanting to give up. We may need to find support to keep moving, both from God and from other people.

Ask Yourself

- Am I able to "press on" and keep moving forward when things get in the way?

- Have I given up on my goals or things that I feel passionate about?

- Do I have the support I need to keep pressing on? Are there people in my life that are willing to help?

- How is God part of my ability to press on?

Bible Passage

"I press on toward the goal for the prize of the upward call of God in Christ Jesus" (Phil. 3:14 ESV).

We are God's handy work, created in Christ Jesus, to do good works" (Eph. 2:10).

Time to Reflect

A Story to be Told
Day 17

We all have a story that can impact others. Sojourner had her story formally written, and it sold well, helping people to understand her mission.

In the same year the Fugitive Slave Act was passed, Sojourner finished dictating her autobiography to her friend, Olive Gilbert. Olive had taken a liking to Sojourner and was fascinated by her story. Olive had also heard that Frederick Douglass had written his story and was selling the book, so she encouraged Sojourner to do the same.

Sojourner appreciated that someone was interested in her life, but she never learned to read or write. Olive offered to help and took dictation over several years. She additionally helped with the publication of the book entitled, *The Narrative of Sojourner Truth, A Northern Slave*. William Lloyd Garrison, a well-known journalist and abolitionist, wrote the preface.

Along with her talks, she became widely known for her book. Sojourner received unprecedented recognition in a world where women were not highly regarded, especially black women. The book sold well and helped to support Sojourner; it also opened doors for more opportunities to speak.

Think Today

We come from generations passed, where we as

African Americans had little value. We were bought and sold just like any other property, and our lives were insignificant, our stories hardly mattered.

The telling of Sojourner's story began to change that. With the writing and publication of her story, she made a statement that all people, even poor black slaves, were important, deserved freedom, and deserved to be heard. She left a legacy that changed things for the generations that came after her and allowed us to think differently about who we are in society and our inherent worth. Our stories matter and Sojourner laid the groundwork for that to be the case.

Ask Yourself

- Do I have a story to tell? Is it connected to a dream God has given me for my life?

- Do I think my story has value?

- How do I tell my story? Do I tell it like I am a victim with bad things always happening to me, or do I talk about how I have overcome my challenges?

- Can my story be an inspiration for others?

Bible Passage

"And the Lord answered me: 'Write the vision; make it plain on tablets, so he may run who reads it'" (Hab. 2:2).

Recognizing Process will reveal your potential. The process of trying the potential is revealed.

Time to Reflect

Opportunities to Prosper
Day 18

Everyone has the desire to do well and prosper. Sojourner prospered in her work and life when she followed her passion and let herself be guided by God and supported by others.

Sojourner was becoming more and more popular as a speaker, building relationships, and selling her books. Many of those who supported her were well-known abolitionists who would invite her on speaking tours with them. George Thompson, a member of the British Royal Parliament, heard about Sojourner and asked her to join him on several speaking engagements. William Lloyd Garrison, who had written the preface to her book, invited Sojourner to speak in Rhode Island, Massachusetts, and New York in early 1851. Sojourner was so appreciative of how these kind men treated her.

On her travels, she met many other people who supported her work and purchased her books. Amy and Isaac Post, Quakers from Rochester, New York, were especially supportive of Sojourner and of promoting book sales. The money she made from both speaking and her book sales allowed her to pay her bills and save money for the future. Overall, the early 1850s was a wonderful time of prosperity for Sojourner.

Think Today

We are all given opportunities to prosper. One reason Sojourner was able to do so well is that she listened to and followed God's guidance, and He brought people into her life that could help. She opened the door to these people, and the opportunities followed.

When opportunity knocks, you can open the door, or you can leave it shut. Not all doors are meant to be opened. And part of prospering is knowing when to seize an opportunity and when to walk away. Sojourner asked for God's guidance in knowing who to trust and which opportunities to take. Knowing when to open a door and when to shut it can be challenging.

Opportunities to prosper are waiting for you! Many people come in and out of our lives. It helps to pay attention to the true essence of why someone is there. Sometimes it is purposeful, and other times, it can be a whole lot of drama.

On our journey, as we focus on our mission and follow the guidance that comes, the right doors will open. These doors hold the possibility of opportunities to receive God's riches.

Ask Yourself

- When opportunities present themselves, am I able to trust and move forward?

- Do I sometimes close the door out of fear?

- Have I asked for God's help in finding opportunities and trusting they will help me prosper?

- Can I look back and see a pattern of help that has been there for me? Or do I close my eyes to the help and opportunities that God sends?

Bible Passage

"I know your deeds. Behold, I have put before you an open door which no one can shut, because you have a little power, and have kept My word, and have not denied my name" (Rev. 3:8).

Time to Reflect

Barriers Must Come Down
Day 19

Sojourner's life was a testament to finding ways to take down barriers. She saw what was in the way, and passionately tackled it. She fought for freedom and equal rights for all.

Sojourner was a hardworking woman of dignity; she boldly stood her ground and advocated for that in which she believed. Although she encountered many barriers, she worked continually to push through them. Her work in general, was based on the need for barriers to come down for others: Barriers to freedom, barriers to equal rights, and barriers for women emancipation.

Her most famous speech occurred in Akron, Ohio, in 1851 before the Woman's Rights Convention. The speech entitled *Ain't I a Woman?* Was delivered to an audience of mostly women, but challenged men. "If my cup would hold a pint and yours a quart, wouldn't it be mean, not to let me have my measure full?" She asked the audience.

Sojourner made numerous points about men and women being equal in the eyes of God. She tried to discredit the idea that men were superior because Jesus was a man. This barrier needed to come down in Sojourner's estimation. "Where did Christ come from?" she asked her audience.
"From God and a woman, man had nothing to do with it." She informed the women before her. This talk was

very well received. Sojourner was given credit for helping take down barriers and helping people see another side to the argument, that maybe God did not intend for women to be lesser.

Think Today

Barriers always exist between two things, in Sojourner's case between the right to freedom and the lack of freedom, the right for women to vote, or the inability to vote. The people of Sojourner's time could have lived with the barriers placed in front of them, but they chose to fight to overcome the barriers between them and freedom, and between them and equal rights for women.

Whether we choose to go beyond the barriers in our lives or stay behind them, we need to be purposeful and take them down. We must ask ourselves; do I knock them down with a purpose? Do I have a vision of what lies beyond my barriers? Do I vote during voting season?

Ask Yourself

- What barriers are in my life right now? Am I trying to take them down?

- Am I stuck in my circumstances and looking for a way out?

- Do I ask for help from God or others to remove my barriers?

- Am I hiding behind the barrier(s)?

Bible Passage

"The one who breaks open will come up before them; they will break out, pass through the gate, and go out by it their king will pass before them, with the Lord at the head" (Mic. 2:13 NIV).

Time to Reflect

_____
_____
_____
_____
_____
_____
_____
_____
_____
_____
_____
_____
_____

Selfless Love and the Willingness to Serve
Day 20

Sojourner embodied the way God would have us live: in service to others. She lived her life with a focus on what she could give and how she could help.

In September of 1857, Sojourner sold all her possessions and moved to Battle Creek, Michigan, where several of her daughters lived. She resided in nearby Harmonia for ten years, while also traveling and working on the east coast. Information from the 1860 census shows that her daughter Elizabeth and two grandsons lived with her at the time.

At the beginning of the American Civil War, in 1861, Sojourner gathered supplies for black volunteer regiments. She continued to volunteer throughout the Civil War in support of the black soldiers who were in segregated squadrons. Although black soldiers were not treated the same as white soldiers, they were able to fight in the war.

The unfair treatment, however, was at times, repulsive and motivated Sojourner to help even more. She gathered together her community in Battle Creek and prepared a Thanksgiving feast for the black soldiers stationed nearby. She served the food and amused the men with her singing. She spoke to them while they ate, and her words of encouragement touched their hearts. They thanked her with loud cheers and applause for all her kindness and selfless love.

Think Today

Being in service for others can be a way of life. In all circumstances, we are either in service for others or in service for ourselves. God would have us be in service for others. And that is why Jesus said, "Anyone who wants to be first must be the very last, and the servant of all" (Mark 9:35).

It is difficult to be an example of kindness and selfless love the way Sojourner was. It takes work and sacrifice but also has its rewards. It is a higher calling to give to others and look for nothing in return. By serving others, by looking out for your brothers and sisters, you can experience greatness in your own life.

Ask Yourself

- Do I understand the importance of selfless love and caring for others first?

- Have I thought about how I can serve my community?

- When was the last time I volunteered?

- Am I willing to forgo my needs to help others?

Bible Passage

"For even the Son of Man did not come to be served, but to serve and to give his life as a ransom for many" (Mark 10:45)

Time to Reflect

_____

_____

_____

_____

_____

_____

_____

_____

_____

_____

_____

_____

_____

_____

_____

_____

Speaking Out Against Injustice
Day 21

Sojourner had many opportunities to speak out against the injustices faced by black slaves in the United States. Many of these opportunities required considerable personal risk on her part.

In 1864, Sojourner went to Washington DC to work for the National Freedman's Relief Association and help freed slaves. She visited the White House and met President Abraham Lincoln. The Civil War was still going on, and she spoke with the President about that and about her desire to see all slaves freed. She noticed he seemed stressed, and she counseled him, speaking freely about injustice. "You remind me of Daniel in the lion's den, but with God's help, you will win this battle." She had no shame in speaking about God to him or anyone. Lincoln was grateful for her words and signed her book of life, "For Aunty Sojourner Truth."

Sojourner enjoyed visiting Washington and wanted to help as much as possible with the Union war effort. She met a well-known black minister, Henry Highland Garnet, who invited her to speak at a fundraiser to help black soldiers. She also worked in a local hospital giving aid to escaped slaves. At great peril to herself, she spoke out about the injustice of the slave traders who were kidnapping blacks and taking them back to Confederate states.

In 1865, she was asked to be a counselor for former slaves who lived in a camp in Arlington Heights, Virginia. She was then appointed to an administrative position in the Freedmen's Hospital in Washington, DC. In all these positions, she fought against the poor conditions and injustices faced by blacks. She always gave credit to God for her strength in the face of adversity, and doors were regularly opened for her.

Think Today

Speaking out against injustice may be uncomfortable for you, but ignoring it makes you a victim. Speaking out against the injustices you see around you is scary, but also empowering. Sojourner found the strength to speak out because she saw herself as a soldier of God, doing God's work to right the wrongs around her. She knew God had her back and would keep her safe. This relationship between her and God held true over and over in her work.

When you know God has your back, you have nothing to fear, and you can focus on doing the right thing. Our job as servants of God on Earth, is to work on righting the wrongs around us. Your fight may be very personal to you, as we are all called to make a difference in different ways. Allowing yourself to be open to God's wisdom through a personal relationship with Him can make all the difference in speaking out against injustice. You can rest assured that, "If you don't stand for something, you will fall for anything." Let justice be served.

Ask Yourself

- Have I given thought to where I see injustice around me?

- Am I silent when it comes to speaking out against injustice?

- Do I believe that God has my back? Even if I were to start speaking out about the truth?

- On my journey, are my eyes open, or am I in denial of what is going on around me?

Bible Passage

"Righteousness and justice are the foundation of your throne; steadfast love and faithfulness go before you." (Ps. 89:14).

Time to Reflect

Breaking Ground
Day 22

The accomplishment of her lifelong dream of ending slavery could have been an endpoint for Sojourner, but instead, it became an opportunity to break new ground.

In April of 1865, while Sojourner was still working in Virginia, President Abraham Lincoln was shot and killed while attending a play at the Ford Theatre. In Washington, D.C. Sojourner was devastated by his death, both at the loss of him as a person and at the loss of his advocacy for ending slavery. At the time, the Civil War was coming to an end, but there was still work that needed to happen before slaves would be free.

Later in 1865, when Confederate armies gave up to the Union and the war ended, a 13th Amendment was added to the Constitution abolishing slavery. This amendment was a monumental achievement and something Sojourner was overwhelmed to see happen during her lifetime. Once again, her prayers had been answered.

Although the battle to end slavery was over, the battle for equality had hardly begun. Many whites hated blacks and resented their freedom. Although Sojourner was happy to see that slavery was finally over, she did not stop there; she kept moving forward, breaking new ground in gaining more rights for the freed slaves.

Think Today

With every ending, there is a chance for a new beginning: the opportunity to break ground on something new. This opportunity might be the continuation of something or an entirely new direction. Sojourner was immediately able to see that although slavery was over, there were new battles to be fought for blacks to be on an equal footing with whites.

In all our lives, there are times when we are conclude things. It can be finishing a great accomplishment or even letting go of a dream unfulfilled. When something is completed, we have the opportunity to build something new. Anything we build in our lives starts just like constructing a house or a building. You begin by breaking ground, digging, and making way for a new edifice. You might even put up a sign that tells of this new venture (coming soon).

Breaking ground is an exciting time filled with new possibilities. Things may go as planned as you dig into new territory, or you may hit a rock or hard place that stops you from digging or breaks your focus. Being discouraged or disappointed is part of the process, but you must not let it stop you from continuing to break that new ground. "Sow for yourselves righteousness, reap the fruit of unfailing love, and **break up your unplowed ground**; for it is time to seek the Lord, until he comes and showers righteousness on you" (Hosea 10:12). Fulfill your dream.

Ask Yourself

- Where am I concluding things in my life?

- What kind of new ground do I want to break?

- Do I allow others to determine what my dreams and goals ought to look like?

- What do I see as obstacles to building something new?

Bible Passage

"For with God, nothing shall be impossible" (Luke 1:37).

Time to Reflect

A Test of Character
Day 23

In breaking new ground, Sojourner took on the fight for segregated seating for blacks on public transportation. She wanted blacks to have the same rights and privileges as whites. She tried several times to change things by organizing protests.

During one of her many protests against segregation, Sojourner asserted her character and stood right in front of a streetcar to stop it. She wanted to make a statement and was determined to put the segregation law to the test. She yelled to the public, "I want to ride; I want to ride."

People standing around and watching laughed and cheered. When she got on the trolley and sat in the white section, the trolley driver became angry and told her to move to the black section, or she would have to get off. Sojourner responded by saying, "I will sit wherever I choose; I know my rights!" and surprisingly, the trolley driver backed off and continued driving the trolley.

Sojourner laid the foundation for the work of the civil rights movement. She demonstrated that by her steadfast character how to stand your ground and inspired people who came after her like Rosa Parks. Almost 90 years later, Rosa Parks took a seat in the white section on a still segregated bus in the South as a protest against inequality and became a hero for human rights.

Think Today

What makes a person who they are? Your character and personality combine to determine who you are. Character can be comprised of positive attributes like integrity, trustworthiness, honesty, patience, and responsibility. It can also be composed of negative attributes like dishonesty, unfaithfulness, and selfishness. Character traits are formed, and the strength of our character matters. Our character is built up through a series of tests that life hands us, which we must decide how to respond to. Do we take the high road and respond with goodness and caring like Sojourner, or do we take the low road and respond in ways that only benefit ourselves?

Sojourner and Rosa had differences in their personality, but both had the strength of character. Imagine if you were living during either of their timeframes and facing challenges as they faced. Being black could mean routinely being treated with disrespect, even humiliated in front of others. It would not have been easy for these women to have stood up to the unfair social rules of their times.

Ask Yourself

- How would I describe my character? What attributes best describe me?

- Am I a good model of integrity working to make positive changes in my community?

- How do I act when others are engaging in negative behavior? Do I join them or set a better example?

- When my character is tested, do I show the strength of character by doing the right thing?

Bible Passage

"Show yourself in all respects to be a model of good works, and in your teaching show integrity, dignity, and sound speech that cannot be condemned, so that an opponent may be put to shame, having nothing evil to say about us" (Tit.2:7-8 ESV).

Time to Reflect

Be A Problem Solver
Day 24

Life will always hold a series of challenges. Sojourner understood this and vowed to tackle problems as they came.

In 1867, Sojourner gave an address to the American Equal Rights Association, urging people to address the problem of equal rights for women, especially black women. At this point, the opposition to her crusade had died down, because she was well established and had built a reputation as a problem solver. She had many opportunities for speaking engagements because she was willing to tackle hard questions and look for solutions. During her speech for the American Equal Rights Association, she kept stressing the need to keep things going while the momentum was strong. She believed that solutions would definitely come. Striking while the iron is hot, so to speak, was one of her problem-solving strategies.

Sojourner was a problem solver by nature, and she found resolving problems as a kind of antidote to the pain she had endured. If all that she had suffered could be put right by giving freedom and equality to others, well, then it was worth it to her.

Another way Sojourner approached problem-solving was to get people to think. In her 1867 speech, she used Bible scriptures to back up her message on equal rights and challenged men to examine their perspectives, saying, "Man is so selfish that he has got women's rights and his own too, and yet he won't give women their rights. He keeps them all to himself." She got people talking and thinking and moving towards a solution.

Think Today

Sometimes in life, we let problems overwhelm us rather than see them as an opportunity to make progress. Problems are not always bad, and many times, they open doors to new and wonderful things. Many men of Sojourner's era were mortified at the thought of women voting, and women wanting the vote became a huge problem. Men thought women were not smart enough to vote, but look at what happened. When they did get the vote, the world did not fall apart, and they were also able to contribute intellectually, making significant discoveries in medicine and science, and contributing exceptional pieces to literature.

Sojourner would have said that problems offer new opportunities, and that society needs to keep growing and evolving. Problems can provide opportunities to shift our perspectives, to understand how we feel, to clarify things in our lives, and ultimately to make things better. It is crucial to think about how we as individuals, approach problems, and if we can see God's hand in the challenges that come to us.

Ask Yourself

- Am I a problem solver? Or am I waiting for someone else to solve my problems?

- What do I do when I am in a problematic situation?

- Do I ask for God's guidance in solving problems?

- Have I ever been recognized for the work I have done in solving a problem?

Bible Passage

"I can do all things through Him who strengthens me" (Phil. 4:13).

Time to Reflect

Feeling Privilege
Day 25

Sojourner experienced more than one challenges while riding on a streetcar. She came face to face with white privilege and stood her ground.

Several years after her famous protest in 1865, Sojourner Truth was again discriminated against by the driver of a trolley. She was with a white friend, Laura Haviland, and when the trolley stopped, Sojourner quickly jumped on ahead of Laura. The driver immediately shoved Sojourner aside and said, "Move, let this woman on first, referring to Laura." Sojourner announced, "I am a woman too."

A white male passenger then confronted the driver, saying, "Why are Negros allowed on this trolley?" The driver told Sojourner to get off, but she refused. She would not move, and Laura told Sojourner to come and take a seat. The driver questioned Laura asking, "Does she belong to you?" Laura said, "No, she belongs to humanity." The driver then aggressively pushed Sojourner and dislocated her shoulder. After the incident, Sojourner sued the driver for assault. Not only did Sojourner win her case, but the driver lost his job.

Think Today

Even as freed slaves gained rights, they were still discriminated against, and many people maintained an attitude of white privilege. The truth is we all have prejudices and discriminate against something or someone, sometimes. It is a part of our nature that needs overcoming, but privilege exists in our culture, our institutions, and even in our churches.

What makes a person think that they are better than another person or that their race is better than another race? People discriminate based on a feeling of superiority, and it may target race, ethnicity, disability, intellectual ability, looks, religion, political preference, and more. Some people are stuck in their preconceived ideas and get gratification from asserting privilege over others, just like the man who did not want Sojourner on the trolley because of her skin color.

When a person thinks he or she is superior to another that is called arrogance. Arrogance is a form of pride, and "pride goes before a fall." Let your goal be to learn to let go of superior attitudes and disagree without discrimination. Ask the question, "What would Jesus do?" and be a representation of his service to others with humility.

Ask Yourself

- Is there somewhere in my life that I experienced discrimination?

- Have I stood up for myself and confronted any prejudice? Have I worked or volunteered on human rights for others?

- Do I feel that I am superior to others or hold superior attitudes?

- When I see someone being discriminated against, do I speak up?

Bible Passage

"Let love be without dissimulation. Abhor that which is evil; cleave to that wish is good. Be kindly affectioned one to another with brotherly love, in honor preferring one another" (Rom. 12: 9-10 KJV).

Time to Reflect

Citizenship
Day 26

Citizenship is a type of belonging. It grants you rights as part of a group but also expects things from you. Sojourner fought for blacks and women to belong fully.

Even though the 13th Amendment had been ratified, and slaves were now free, they were not allowed to be citizens or have those rights: this was another battleground for Sojourner. Arguments raged about who should be granted citizenship. Should white women be first? Should black men be granted these rights and not black women? Sojourner worried that if black men were allowed to become citizens, it would leave black women feeling like slaves all over again.

In 1868, the 14th Amendment was ratified, granting citizenship to everyone born or naturalized in the United States, and granting them rights and protections under the law. However, there were still Jim Crow laws forcing segregation throughout the South, and the reality of equal rights was a long way off.

Sojourner's fight for citizenship shifted to a fight for equal voting rights. Blacks and white women were marginalized in society in many ways and still did not have the right to vote.
Sojourner was good at constructing arguments against the rationale white men used to exclude others. One such argument was that women did not have much intellect. "What's intellect got to do with women's

rights or negro rights?" Sojourner rebuked the argument and drew strong comparisons between the restraints on women's rights and the way masters treated slaves.

Think Today

Some might say that Sojourner's struggles are in the past and not relevant today.
There are, however, many lessons to be learned from Sojourner's journey that are applicable today. If you think about the hardships and stressful conditions she endured, wouldn't you agree that people today, whether white, Latino, black, or Asian, are fighting some of the same battles? Citizenship, equal opportunities, poverty, and contemporary forms of slavery like human trafficking, and the school-toprison pipeline have plagued our modern world.

We have come so far, but we are still fighting for equality and working to break the mental chains of slavery that have taken up residence in our psyches. Citizenship grants you rights in theory, but not always in practice.

God brought us out of slavery, and we can overcome our disadvantages through the blessing of God's resources. See yourself as a son or daughter of God and claim your citizenship in this world.

Ask Yourself

- What does citizenship mean to me? Have I given any real thought to what a blessing it is?

- Where around me do I see inequality for people of different races or sexes?

- Do I advocate for change where I see these inequalities?

- Have you considered what it is like for people around you who do not have citizenship and how you might help?

Bible Passage

"Be a good citizen. All governments are under God. Insofar as there is peace and order, it is God's order" (Rom. 13:1 Message Bible).

So, live responsibly as a citizen. If you are irresponsible to the state, then you are irresponsible with God, and God will hold you responsible.

Time to Reflect

Gaining Territory
Day 27

Sojourner's life was consistently focused on gaining more rights for those oppressed. She set an example of how to stay focused and gain territory even as she was advancing in age.

Later in 1868, Sojourner had an opportunity to meet with President Ulysses S. Grant. Grant was the former commander of the Union armies and was open to her passionate concerns about blacks living in poverty in the South and their need for education. Sojourner thanked him for his efforts to secure guarantees of justice for blacks. He told her that everyone deserves equal rights. He further signed one of her books, and she left him with one of her calling cards as a souvenir.

By this time, Sojourner was over 70 years old. After meeting with President Grant, she began meeting with senators and congressmen about supporting former slaves with land grants. They told her that she needed a formal petition letter to propose more changes. A senator named Charles Summer, an abolitionist in support of Sojourner, suggested she start touring and speaking to get support from the people. She traveled to many states, speaking out about the injustice blacks were still suffering and gathering signatures for land grants and voting rights for black settlers in the western states.

Congress ratified the 15th Amendment at the start of 1870. This amendment guaranteed the right to vote to all men regardless of "race, color, or previous conditions of servitude." The right to vote was crucial to the welfare of blacks, who made up a sizable portion of the southern population and composed the majority in some states. This law stirred people up, and white supremacist groups such as the Ku Klux Klan went about kidnapping and killing blacks in response. President Grant sent federal troops to South Carolina and other troubled areas to restore order.

Think Today

Sojourner advocated over a long period and well into her senior years. She saw incredible gains in territory. Laws were passed, and things changed in favor of black Americans. Segregation, however, was still an issue, especially in transportation, drinking fountains, and places of entertainment. Blacks were not able to sit side-by-side with whites, especially in the South. Sojourner's success in gaining new territory lay in part to the fact that she looked forward and did not dwell on what was not working but on how to reach the next goal. She likely felt discouraged at times, but she never gave up.

Take a moment to think of your journey and where you have gained new territory. Does doubt creep in? Does it stop you? Sojourner was able to remain steadfast because she had trust in God. She knew God would bring her through tough times, and He would show her the way. God is there for all of us, and God has a plan for how to gain territory in each of our lives.

Ask Yourself

- What skills do I have that can help make positive changes in the world? Can I speak, write, build homes or pass out food?

- Where am I called to fight for change and expand into new territory?

- What am I doing to see this happen?

- What is in the way of my future endeavors? Do I have enough trust in God?

Bible Passage

"Now Jabez called on the God of Israel, saying, "Oh that You would bless me indeed and enlarge my borders, and that your hand might be with me, and that You would keep me from harm that it may not pain me! And God granted him what he requested" (1 Chr 4:10 KJV).

T

Time to Reflect

Taking Care of Ourselves So We Can Take Care of Others
Day 28

Sojourner was tireless in her efforts to create change. In her days, no one talked about selfcare, but without recharging, we cannot be of good service to others.

In the early 1870s, Sojourner was still traveling to get signatures on petitions. She took her grandson, Sammy Banks, with her; he was a great help to her because he could read. He was also a great source of comfort and companion. In 1874, they traveled together to Washington D.C. to deliver petitions to Congress. Sojourner was still working on various forms of land grants for freed slaves, to establish a means for them to better support themselves.

Travel was hard in this era, and by this time, Sojourner was in her mid-70s and not a young woman. After taking the petitions to Washington, they returned to Battle Creek, Michigan, where Sojourner had purchased a home. Her grandson became ill, and she nursed him for a time but developed ulcers on her legs and became incapacitated herself. They did clear up, but then she also fell ill. Although she did recover, the illness took its toll.
Sammy Banks died while having an operation shortly after, and Sojourner battled both her recovery and her grief before she was able to once again set off on her mission to help freed slaves.

Think Today

No one can just give and give and give without replenishing themselves. Sojourner was tireless in her work, but she needed to balance taking care of herself with all the energy she put into her advocacy. On top of that, losing someone she loved and cared for, added additional strain.

It is so vital to take care of ourselves and our bodies. Living with stress is a normal part of our lives, but we must balance out the stress with loving kindness to ourselves. God would have us love and care for ourselves as well as others. We need to learn to both work hard and stop to be still and to rest.

Ask Yourself

- Do I work too hard? Do I give all my energy away to others?

- Am I listening to my body? What are my illnesses and maladies telling me?

- Do I take time to exercise and get the proper amount of rest for my body?

- Do I take care of myself first so that I can be there to take care of others?

Bible Passage

"Or do you not know that your body is the temple of the Holy Spirit who is in you, whom you have from God, and you are not your own" (1 Cor. 6:19 NKJV).

Time to Reflect

Being Who You Are
Day 29

God only requires one thing of us, and that is to be true to who we are. In being ourselves, we can naturally share the love and gifts that God has bestowed on us. Sojourner and her counterpart Harriet Tubman were great examples of this.

Sojourner Truth is often mistaken for Harriet Tubman because they were both famous black women who fought for the abolition of slavery. Although they have many things in common, they did things very differently. Sojourner Truth, named Isabella Baumfree by her parents, lived from 1797-1883. Harriet Tubman, named Araminta Ross by her parents, lived from 1826-1913. These two women overlapped in their lives and work and knew each other.

Both of these women have the distinction of being former slaves who gained their freedom, both changed their names, and both fought hard to free slaves. They both left a legacy that has been written about and ultimately, they both changed history. You might think this makes them similar, but the commonality ends there.

Sojourner was different from Harriet Tubman in appearance, personality, and method of fighting slavery. Sojourner Truth was over six feet tall and slim, while Tubman was a foot shorter and stout. Sojourner dressed in the Quaker style, a white bonnet worn on the head, lightweight dresses, and a shawl over her shoulders. Harriet Tubman wrapped a bandana around her head, her dresses were made of coarse heavy cotton, and she did not wear a shawl. Sojourner had a long face, wore metal-rimmed eyeglasses, and was a commanding figure. Harriet Tubman had a broad full face, wore no eyeglasses, and was unassuming.

They also differed in personality. Sojourner was an obedient slave who saw her owner as god-like and believed he could read her mind. Even when beaten, she was always willing to please him. Sojourner was a patient person who did not complain about the injustice of being a slave. In contrast, Tubman was not submissive and fought back when beaten by her owner. She spoke out and had no patience for slavery.

Their advocative work differed in style also. Sojourner looked at the big picture of slavery and understood it would take time for all the slaves to be freed. She believed slavery could be ended peacefully by moral persuasion. She became a willing activist, giving antislavery speeches at abolition meetings and women's rights conventions to build sentiment against the institution of slavery. Unlike Sojourner, Harriet Tubman undertook a personal crusade against slavery.
She worked on devising ways of helping slaves escape and worked extensively with the Underground Railroad. Sojourner fought the system, Tubman worked around it.

Think Today

A study of these two women reminds us that there is not just one way to do things. Some people see the big picture and work on systemic change; others function more directly helping people get their needs met now. No one way of doing things is better than the other; they both serve an important purpose. Like actors in a play, everyone has a role and all roles matter.

Ultimately, both Sojourner Truth and Harriet Tubman succeeded because they were committed to being themselves. They both listened to the voice of God to direct their path. God made us who we are, and we do not have to be anyone else or do things differently than how we do them. Being ourselves and being true to who we are is the right way for each of us. "I will praise You, for I am
fearfully and wonderfully made; Marvelous are Your works, and that my soul knows very well." (Psa. 139:14).

Ask Yourself

- Am I willing to be myself and not feel the need to act like someone else?

- Am I telling the truth about who I am and what I believe? Can I do this in all circumstances and with all people?

- If not, what stops me?

- Do I feel I have to pretend to be someone other than who I am? Why?

Bible Passage

"Having gifts that differ according to the grace given to us, let us use them: if prophecy, in proportion to our faith; if service, in our serving; the one who teaches, in his teaching" (Rom. 12:6-7 ESV)

Time to Reflect

Breaking the Chains of Trauma

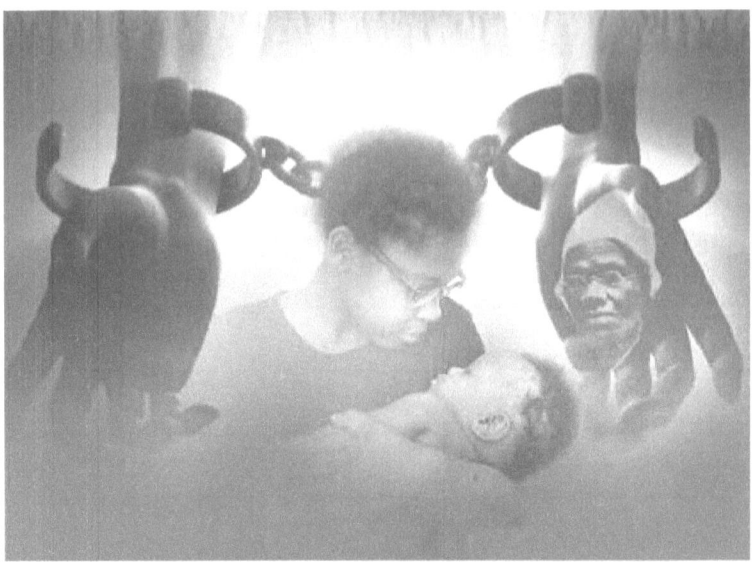

Photo by Tanesha Shipp

"I am pleading for my people, a poor downtrodden race
Who dwell in freedom's boasted land with no abiding place
I am pleading that my people may have their rights restored,
For they have long been toiling and yet had no reward They are
forced the crops to culture, but not for them they yield,
although both late and early, they labor in the field.
While I bear upon my body, the scores of many a gash, I'm
pleading for my people who groan beneath the lash. I'm
pleading for the mothers who gaze in wild despair
Upon the hated auction block and see their children there.
I feel for those in bondage—well may I feel for them.
I know how fiendish hearts that can be sell their fellow men. Yet
those oppressors steeped in guilt—I still would have them live; For
I have learned of Jesus, to suffer and forgive!
I want no carnal weapons, no machinery of death.
For I love to not hear the sound of war's tempestuous breath.
I do not ask you to engage in death and bloody strife.
I do not dare insult my God by asking for their life. But
while your kindest sympathies to foreign lands do roam, I
ask you to remember your own oppressed at home.
I plead with you to sympathize with signs and groans and scars,
And note how base the tyranny beneath the stripes and stars."

Olive Gilbert & Sojourner Truth (1878), *Narrative of Sojourner Truth, a Bondswoman of Olden Time* 1878.

Breaking the Chains
Day 30

Sojourner left a legacy of broken chains. Slaves were no longer chained to owners, blacks were no longer chained to poverty, and the mental chains that constrained our country regarding inequality were loosening.

On November 26, 1883, at the age of 86, Sojourner Truth died at her home in Battle Creek, Michigan. She had outlived all her children, and the Civil War's fight to free slaves was long behind her. African Americans, however, were still trying to free themselves from the physical and psychological scars of slavery, and a woman's right to vote would not be achieved for another thirty-seven years. Race and gender inequality would continue indefinitely.

Sojourner was inducted into the National Women's Hall of Fame in Seneca Falls, New York, in 1981. Her story had long ago become famous, along with other women like Elizabeth Cady, Lucretia Mott, and Susan B. Anthony, who fought for women's rights. A statute of Sojourner was erected in her hometown of Battle Creek, Michigan, in 1997, over 100 years after her death.

At the end of her life, if she did look back, Sojourner would have been proud of all she accomplished in advancing the lives of blacks and women. She worked on changing the way people saw things and created a new normal. Through ongoing self-sacrifice, her willingness to take risks, speak her mind, trust in God, and ultimately forgive, enabled her to accomplish most of what she set out to do. Sojourner succeeded in her mission to spread God's truth: that everyone was equal in his eyes. She told her story and led the way to freedom. Her dying words were, "Be a follower of the Lord Jesus."

Think Today

To bring healing, we need to wake up and face the truth. We need to hold people accountable, even when it feels uncomfortable. We need to listen to each other's stories. We need to stand up in the midst of adversity and break the chains of generational trauma. ***"You shall know the truth, and the truth shall make you free" (John 8:32).***

When we look around us, there are still many places where people feel constrained and where there is still inequity throughout our society. Everyone deserves equal rights in America. We should be looking for equality and not revenge.

Our awareness of these inequities is the first step towards changing them.

When we dream of things being better, we are hoping that someday they will come true. Why not now? We all can impact the world around us, to change things for the better, and to make a difference. This is our purpose for being. We were created to live a life that God purposed for us - to serve others and make this world a loving place. That purpose must be fulfilled in this life.

We can achieve that by tapping into God's love, for He is the source of our creative power.

Ask Yourself

- What is God's purpose for me?

- Where can I help change things for the better?

- What creative gifts can I use to achieve my purpose?

- What, from Sojourner's life, can inspire me and help me break the chains in my own life and lineage?

Biblical Passage

"But seek ye first the Kingdom of God, and His righteousness and all these things shall be added unto you" (Matt. 6:33 KJV).

Purpose/Destiny

Reflect for a moment and see your future.

_____
_____
_____
_____
_____
_____
_____
_____
_____
_____
_____
_____
_____
_____

IN CONCLUSION!

Knowledge is power, you can't know where you're going until you know where you've been

There is a beginning to our understanding of God's grace and mercies. He then called us to be reborn in Him. This birth is a new birth to the pathway of maturity, walking it out with God, being an overcomer, and leading a victorious life.

The spiritual journey involves growth in understanding who we are and how we can walk this life out with God. During our walk with Him, He carries us many times.
Then He allows us to walk on our own with the choices we make. There are times we may not hear His voice to take the next step. He's there with arms outstretched, "Lo, I am with you always" bidding us to come (Matthew 28:20). He tells us that our steps are ordered by Him, and when we learn to hear His voice, lean on Him, and follow Him, He will lead us in the right way of life.

Hurt, pain, and trauma experienced over generations without having taken subsequent steps to heal have contaminated our focus as to how we can be real and trust one another.

That includes telling the truth when it hurts and expressing the pain felt.

Conversations need to be about telling our stories until we come to a place of love and peace.

It's easy to go numb and sit in our emotions, hurt, or pain. To bring healing, we will need to have an awakening of the truth. May I say again, hold people accountable, even when it feels uncomfortable. Have open and true conversations. Listen to each one's story. Stand up in times of adversity and break the chains of generational trauma.

Find your voice and speak out against racism and evil.

Racism is rooted in fear, pride, and insecurities. It's a mindset that you may liken to a slave mentality, causing trauma and pain for many. Everyone should have the same rights in America and not separatism, equality and not revenge.

Let us "Break those chains" that keep us stuck. Free yourself! Come, sit down, let us reason together and put differences aside. No person is superior to another. We all have the potential to greatness! Unlock your potential so you can fulfill your purpose! Find your nitch and hook up! Forgive and forget!

"If my people, which are called by my name, shall humble themselves, and pray, and seek my face, and turn from their wicked way; then will I hear from heaven, and will forgive their sin, and heal their land" (2 Chr. 7:14).

Serve with love, kindness, and understanding. We are all in this together.

Birth a new vision, life begins at conception!

IN MEMORY OF SALEEMAH SHABAZZ SALAHUD -DIN

Saleemah was an important part of my life and work from the time she was ten years old to her recent passing at 39 in 2020. A talented and phenomenal woman with a visible zest for life, she shared her love, life, and gifts of speaking and acting with her four children, family, friends, church, and community. Saleemah was a dedicated soldier and faithful servant within Crossroads Panorama (CRP) where she served various roles--as she had done within Actors for Christ (AFC) in earlier years. She will continue to be remembered with love and gratitude as a dear friend. I am now remembering her by celebrating her life.

ABOUT THE AUTHOR

Drama therapist, Dr. Joyce Marrie is the founder and Executive Director of Crossroads Panorama, a community-based arts program that empowers youth and young adults through the arts. Through her work at Crossroads Panorama, Dr. Marrie gives the lifeline to finding purpose, self-worth, and healing by changing old behaviors that hinder creativity.

With her years of experience designing and implementing creative drama programs for youth, Dr. Marrie is a teacher, writer, producer, and consultant. She is the author and publisher of "We're All on a Journey to Find Truth: The Life and History of Sojourner Truth, Volumes 1 and 2," "A Teacher's Guide for Grades 7-12," and "Breaking the Chains of Trauma: A 30-Day Devotional using the Story of Sojourner Truth, Overcoming Generational Trauma Through the Lens of Sojourner Truth."   Dr. Marrie also authored a children's book, "Cherry Wood Finds a Home," which addresses the experience of bullying.

Dr. Marrie presents Sojourner Truth's life through acting and arts to a myriad of audiences, such as educational facilities, traditional and alternative schools, juvenile detention centers, and many community settings. Students learn to use historical events for academic growth and conflict resolution.

BA in Psychology; MA in Human Development. LGSW (Licensed Graduate Social Worker); Mini MBA; and PhD. in Drama and Art Therapy; and RDT (Registered Drama Therapist).

Dr. Marrie is active in her community and received the Richfield Human Rights Commission's Gene and Mary Jacobson Outstanding Citizen Award in 2018. She is also co-chair of the Richfield Arts Commission and serves on the Richfield Community Education Advisory Council.

For ordering "Breaking the Chains of Trauma" or *contact us: chloeartspublishing@gmail.com*

Bibliography

Painter, Neil Irvin. (1997). Sojourner Truth: A Life, A Symbol. New York: Norton

Sankofa

www.ingramcontent.com/pod-product-compliance
Lightning Source LLC
Chambersburg PA
CBHW022105160426
43198CB00008B/365